PIPELINE

PIPELINE

DOMINIQUE MORISSEAU

THEATRE COMMUNICATIONS GROUP   NEW YORK   2018

Pipeline is published by Theatre Communications Group, Inc.,
520 Eighth Avenue, 24th Floor, New York, NY 10018-4156

The publication of *Pipeline* by Dominique Morisseau, through TCG's Book Program, is made possible in part by the New York State Council on the Arts with the support of Governor Andrew Cuomo and the New York State Legislature.

TCG books are exclusively distributed to the book trade by Consortium Book Sales and Distribution.

ISBN 978-1-55936-587-1 (paperback)
ISBN 978-1-55936-902-2 (ebook)
A catalog record for this book is available from the Library of Congress.

Book design and composition by Lisa Govan
Cover design by Monet Cogbill
Cover image by James McMullan

First Edition, September 2018

This play is for my mother, a master-educator and proud public school teacher for forty years in Highland Park, Michigan.

This isn't her story. It's just a similar world in which she was a fiercely committed educator, and worked very hard to help her students transcend.

I salute you, Mama.

Love, Dominique ☺

PIPELINE

PRODUCTION HISTORY

Pipeline was commissioned by Chicago's Steppenwolf Theatre Company (Martha Lavey, Artistic Director; David Hawkanson, Executive Director).

Pipeline received its world premiere on July 10, 2017, at Lincoln Center Theater (André Bishop, Producing Artistic Director, Adam Siegel, Managing Director) in New York City. It was directed by Lileana Blain-Cruz; the scenic design was by Matt Saunders, the costume design was by Montana Levi Bianco, the lighting design was by Yi Zhao, the sound design was by Justin Ellington, the projection design was by Hannah Wasileski; the stage manager was Charles M. Turner III. The cast was:

NYA	Karen Pittman
OMARI	Namir Smallwood
JASMINE	Heather Velazquez
XAVIER	Morocco Omari
LAURIE	Tasha Lawrence
DUN	Jaime Lincoln Smith

CHARACTERS

NYA, Black woman, mid-late thirties. Single mother. Public high school teacher. Trying to raise her teenage son on her own with much difficulty. A good teacher inspiring her students in a stressed environment. A struggling parent doing her damnedest. Strong but burning out. Smoker. Sometimes drinker. Holding together by a thread.

OMARI, Black man, late teens. Smart and astute. Rage without release. Tender and honest at his core. Something profoundly sensitive amidst the anger. Wrestling with his identity between private school education and being from a so-called urban community. Nya's son.

JASMINE, Black or Latina woman, late teens. Sensitive and tough. A sharp bite, a soft smile. Profoundly aware of herself and her environment. Attends upstate private school but from a so-called urban environment. In touch with the poetry of her own language.

XAVIER, Black man, mid-late thirties. Single father, struggling to connect to his own son. Marketing executive. Wounded relationship with his ex-wife. Financially stable. Emotionally impoverished. Nya's ex-husband, Omari's father.

LAURIE, White woman, fifties. Pistol of a woman. Teaches in public high school and can hold her own against the tough students and the stressed environment. Doesn't bite her tongue. A don't-fuck-with-me chick.

DUN, Black man, early-mid-thirties. Public high school security guard. Fit and optimistic. Charismatic with women. Genuine and thoughtful and trying to be a gentleman in a stressed environment. It's not easy.

NOTE ABOUT THE SETTING

Not necessarily New York City, but definitely modeled after it. Can be any inner city environment where the public school system is under duress. However, the quick pace of the language is New York City–inspired and should be maintained in any setting. Present day.

Also, we have undefined space. This is a place where location doesn't matter. It is sometimes an alternate reality bleeding into reality. It is sometimes just isolated reality that doesn't require a setting. Only words.

NOTE ABOUT THE TEXT

A " / " indicates when the next line of dialogue begins.

1

Lights up on Nya. She is on the phone, though we don't have to really see her holding anything. She is living the call.

   As she speaks, images flow behind her: camera-phone video clips of school fights, disjointed and perhaps emerging less into video and more into large overwhelming shadows.

NYA: Hey it's . . . it's me. I know I shouldn't . . . but I don't know what else to . . . we need to talk. It's about our son. He got in a fight. On school grounds. They're going to . . . . they're talking about . . . they're talking kicking him out. They're talking pressing charges. They're going to . . . . I don't know what they're going to . . . . I'm just . . . *(Beat beat beat)* I'm exhausted. You know that? Like there is no more helium. I'm sinking. Like there is all this . . . weight . . . I can't fight gravity. You know? Like I just can't even fight this pulling down . . . taking all of my—I don't know. I don't know. I don't even know. *(Beat beat beat beat beat)*

(Then randomly enthusiastic) So anyway! Give me a call back when you get a moment. So we can talk. Talk about. Your son. Our son. Us . . .

. . .

. . .

(Long, awkward pause.)

Yep. Okay. Bye.

(Quick pause.)

I um . . . I also miss you.

(Beat.)

Fuck. I shouldn't have said that. I'm gonna . . . I should delete that. I'm gonna delete that.

(She pushes a button. We hear the prompt that says: "To erase and rerecord, press 3." She presses 3.
    Then, very professionally:)

Hey, Xavier, it's Nya. Calling to talk to you about our son. Give me a call back when you get this. Thanks. Bye.

(Nya stands in silence for a moment. Then lights a cigarette. She leans her head to the side. Puffs.
    We hear a school bell ring.
    The distant sound of a school day starting. Hallways filled with lockers closing and gossip and trampling feet.
    A public address announcement comes through. It is fast and static:)

PA *(Offstage)*: Good morning students, welcome to another glorious day at Chadsey High. Please remember to take off your hats. No sagging allowed. New policy in effect today—homeroom teachers are now going to lock your cell phones and other non-school-issued devices in their drawers. You will retrieve them at the end of the day. If you have any objections to this, then you are free to leave your devices at home. If you are caught with any non-approved electronic device in class, this is an automatic suspension. No exceptions. I repeat *(Loudly)* NO EXCEPTIONS! Please do not have your mamas coming up here demanding to get your smart phones back. We have the city government behind us. You cannot win. I repeat *(Loudly)* YOU CANNOT WIN! Also, there is a pep rally today after school. Be sure to attend and show your school pride. And finally, have a glorious day, students. *(Loudly)* A GLORIOUS DAY!

(Nya puts her cigarette out on her shoe. Waves the smoke out the window. Then she moves toward a door and opens it.)

NYA: Mornin, class. Pull out your pens. Pop quiz today.

(Groans and sucking teeth are heard. The shadows become harsh fluorescent lights. They bleach us into blindness.)

2

A girl's dormitory. Bedroom.
Jasmine and Omari.

JASMINE: Tell me you wasn't lookin' at her.
OMARI: I wasn't lookin' at her.
JASMINE: Oughta cut her face.
OMARI: I wasn't lookin' at her.
JASMINE: Thinkin' she's so cute.
OMARI: I wasn't lookin' at her.
JASMINE: She ain't that cute.
OMARI: I was kinda lookin' at her.
JASMINE: What?
OMARI: Just like a little bit.
JASMINE: What's a little bit?
OMARI: Like modestly. With no intention. Just observing.
JASMINE: What you got to be observing for?

OMARI: To take in my surroundings. Learn the world. Not be just tied up in my own existence and nothin' else.

JASMINE: Everything's more important to you than me.

OMARI: You important to me.

JASMINE: Not hardly. You just biding your time. Till you figure out what to do next. Ain't that it?

OMARI: Why would you say that?

JASMINE: Cuz I don't like to talk at nothin'. I like to say exactly what's what.

OMARI: You wanna know what's what?

JASMINE: Yeah. I wanna know.

OMARI: I don't know where I'm gonna be two days from now. Or two hours. And I can't be pretending we in some fairy tale fantasy where all I need to do is chill with you in a castle with our horses or whatever.

JASMINE: Horses?

OMARI: Or whatever. I'ono. Whatever they got in castles. Truth is I got too many worries and bein' with you don't make 'em go nowhere. You feel me?

JASMINE: You sayin' I'm addin' to your stress level?

OMARI: I'm sayin' I got stresses. Real ones. And hiding out in your dorm ain't doin' nothin' but prolonging the inevitable.

JASMINE: This some wack version of a breakup?

OMARI: It's just me bein' honest.

JASMINE: Well fuck your honesty. Seriously, Omari, you gonna make my heart explode with all yo' back-and-forthness. One minute you tellin' me I'm the cure. Next minute, I'm the cause. Maybe you your own stress problem and I ain't got nothin' to do with it.

OMARI: Maybe I am.

JASMINE *(Pssshhh)*: Fuck you.

OMARI: Maybe I'm confused.

JASMINE: That's the realest shit you ever said.

(He tugs at her needfully.)

OMARI: Yo, this could be our last time.

(She snatches away.)

JASMINE: You kiddin' me right now?

OMARI: I'm just seeking intimacy.

JASMINE: You seeking to get socked in the eye. I don't turn on and off like no stove.

OMARI: You mean a faucet.

JASMINE: I mean a stove. One minute you got me hot. Next minute fire's out. Quit gassin' me up and killing my fucking spark.

OMARI: Can't nothing kill your spark. You always gon' be fire.

JASMINE: And you always gon' be crazy.

(Beat.)

OMARI *(Truth)*: I'm scared.

(Jasmine looks at him and wants to say something. Then decides against it. She just looks at him with concern.)

JASMINE: Why you fight him, O?

OMARI: Why you say you gonna cut Keely's face?

JASMINE: She thinks she's cute.

OMARI: So you wanna mess that up?

JASMINE: Maybe it would make things balanced.

OMARI: Like what?

JASMINE: Like she wear on the outside what I feel on the inside.

OMARI: That's messed up.

JASMINE: So I'm messed up. *(Beat)* Your moms knows?

OMARI: She probably already planning her speech. Threatening to send me to my pops. But dude wouldn't go for that in a million years.

JASMINE: You ain't supposed to even be here right now. If anybody finds us—

OMARI: Where else can we meet? They won't let me talk to you anywhere on the campus. Supposed to be packing my stuff to go home. Ain't like I could visit you back at your folks' crib. They won't let me nowhere near you.

JASMINE: Teen pregnancy stats got 'em spooked. They have no idea who or what I am.

OMARI: I know what you are.

JASMINE: You don't even know yourself. How you know me?

OMARI: I know you.

JASMINE: What you know?

OMARI: You're a metamorphic rock.

JASMINE: Here you go.

OMARI: What?

JASMINE: Science references from Mr. Peterson's class ain't gonna save you from my wrath.

OMARI: Not trying to get saved. Just makin' an observation.

JASMINE: Explain.

OMARI: Metamorphic rocks. They change in form. Made from heat and pressure. That's what makes 'em so rare and interesting.

JASMINE: And that's me?

OMARI: That's you.

(Jasmine considers this.)

JASMINE: I think I'm in love with you.

OMARI: I think I'm leaving.

JASMINE: Where you goin'?

OMARI: Somewhere else. I got some money saved. Child support stash from the ol' man. Shit adds up when you don't spend it.

JASMINE: You gonna just run from your problems?

OMARI: What else I'm gonna do? Stay and let 'em take away my life? My future?

JASMINE: Maybe not.

OMARI: They recorded it.

JASMINE: So threaten anybody who put it up.

OMARI: I'll never be able to trace it. If it goes viral, I'm a wrap. And it's gonna go viral.

JASMINE: Fuck it then. You'll be a celebrity.

OMARI: I'll be public enemy number one.

JASMINE: You won't.

OMARI: I'll be a monster.

JASMINE: You'll be that motherfucker nobody'll fuck with.

OMARI: That ain't the legacy I was trying to leave.

JASMINE: What legacy you gonna leave now? Runnin' away?

OMARI: I just gotta go, Jasmine.

(Pause.
   They look at each other.
   Jasmine's eyes well up.)

JASMINE: I know what you are.

OMARI: What am I?

JASMINE: A lunar eclipse.

OMARI: How's that?

JASMINE: Rare and hiding in the shadows of the earth. Always ready for an escape.

OMARI: Mr. Peterson's science class is the best.

JASMINE: Don't leave.

OMARI: I think I gotta.

JASMINE: I can't survive this prep shit without you.

OMARI: You can survive anything.

JASMINE: Don't leave.

OMARI: Can I kiss you one last time?

JASMINE: Make it last forever.

(He kisses her. It lasts an eternity.)

3

Teachers' lounge. Afternoon.
Laurie enters. Goes to refrigerator. Pulls out her container.
Puts it in microwave. Sits and waits.
Nya enters and goes to the fridge. Pulls out a salad.

LAURIE: Fucking fifth period.

NYA: You turn in your reports?

LAURIE: Not yet. Humphries is on my ass. English Department head or not—I told him to give me a damn break I only just had my face reconstructed. Asshole.

NYA: You look good, Laurie. I can't even tell.

LAURIE: My husband can. And my daughter. I freak her out, she says. Everything freaks her out that isn't painted with at least a gazillion ounces of mascara. Or liters. Or however the fuck you measure mascara. She's fucking obsessed with it, that's all I know. I mean, what the hell happened to teenage hood? I remember dyeing my hair orange and piercing my nose to rage against the status quo. That was a sort of cause, y'know? But now, it's just all mascara and fashion and next top supermodel housewife of bla bla bla—what the hell are we doing, you know? Are they growing down?

NYA: Probably.

LAURIE: And the substitute was an idiot. I asked my kids what'd they do while I was gone. Three weeks while I was gone. You know nobody could give me a straight answer? Then Alejandro finally cracks. Watched *The Wire*, Season Four— he tells me.

NYA: *The Wire?*

LAURIE: Said the sub was trying to show them what not to do. You fucking kidding me?

NYA: Which sub was this?

LAURIE: The cute young blond straight outta Teachers College. Patricia or Patrice or some shit. What the hell are they teaching them over there? The last sub they sent me showed 'em *Dangerous Minds*. Do they really believe public school is Michelle Pfeiffer and Hilary Swank and corny fucking music and close-ups? I'm a white chick who has never had the luxury of winning over a class full of black and Latino kids. This is war. Got my fucking face cut by the family of a failing student. Fuck them and their lies and the substitutes that show them these dumb-ass, god-forsaken, setting-us-back-three-hundred-educational-years-bullshit flicks. TEACH, you assholes! I left you lesson plans for fuck's sake!

NYA: They should've gotten you Smith. She's a substitute teacher from the gods. When I was gone that week for Omari's pneumonia, I came back and my kids had already moved onto the next chapter of *Invisible Man*. Had their papers graded and everything. Impressive.

LAURIE: An enigma in this place.

NYA: You gonna retire or what?

LAURIE: Fuck them and their retirement. They're not gonna force my hand. Try to move me from ninth grade, to tenth grade, to twelfth. I'll outlast 'em all—bastards.

NYA: You're a pistol, woman.

LAURIE: I'm a goddamn machine gun.

(They pause. Eat for a second.)

How's your son?

NYA: Troubled. Next question.

LAURIE: You figured out what you're gonna do about—

NYA: No. I haven't figured out a thing. I'm slipping off the edge of the earth and there is no answer in the dark dark universe.

LAURIE: The world isn't flat, Nya.

NYA: Mine is, Laurie. It's flat and coming to a quick and fast end. And I can't stop it.

LAURIE: You can. Just got to grab it by the balls and turn it around. That son of yours needs a swift kick in the ass.

NYA: That's not what he needs.

LAURIE: I remember when parents would give permission for you to spank their kids in class. You old enough to remember that?

NYA: We teach teenagers.

LAURIE: Especially the teenagers.

NYA: I don't think I remember that.

LAURIE: That was the best. I'm telling you. I had this one kid, Louie Gaspacho. I remember him real good. You know how some of 'em stay with you for a lifetime. He had kind of a schizophrenia thing going on. Undiagnosed, but I knew. They should let us prescribe the drugs instead of these bogus doctors. I know these kids inside and out. I knew Louie. Another kid I think Ritalin ruined. But his folks listened to that sorry excuse of a counselor, Ms. Esselman—who would recommend a drug to Jesus if she couldn't get him to sit still for five minutes. Never figured maybe it was her tactics and not the kid—but whatever. His folks would never get him tested for his mental health. Couldn't afford the medical bills. Half these damn kids are suffering from mental illness. That's what the real problem is. A classroom can't fix that shit. And neither can Ritalin. But what do they know? Nothing, that's what. I know what these kids need, but who listens to me? Anyway—what the hell was I talking about?

NYA: Louie Gaspacho?

LAURIE: Exactly. He could be a terror if he was really having a day. So one time he threw a book at me. Nearly knocked out the smart little West Indian girl that sat right in front of him—

NYA: Ummm, maybe you shouldn't call her / that.

LAURIE: I grabbed his little scrawny ass in the middle of class and gave him three licks to his backside. Never a book thrown again. That kid got almost straight A's that year. They don't give me my credit for that because he got institutionalized a couple years later and pulled out of school, so it's like he never existed. But I had him functioning high—you know? A good old ass whipping can teach a lot.

NYA: That's not O's problem, Laurie.

LAURIE: I wasn't saying that. I just—

NYA: It's too many things. It's me. I'm the source and I know it and I just can't talk about this anymore if I'm going to get through the rest of the day, okay? Gotta drive upstate to pick him up after work and I'll finish stressing then.

LAURIE: Don't panic, honey. We're all a bunch of screw-ups trying to figure out our mess. You'll figure it out.

NYA: Screw-ups?

LAURIE: Figure of speech. Don't take that literal. It's not literal.

NYA: Right.

(The door to the lounge swings open. Dun enters.)

DUN: Ladies, what it do?

LAURIE: What it do back to ya, you sexy bastard.

DUN: You trying to get me in trouble on school grounds again, Laurie?

LAURIE: Just a little flirtation between a young, hot security guard and a very agile old teacher. Harmless.

DUN: Face lookin' good, girl. Got you all brand-new.

LAURIE: They can't keep a white chick down.

DUN: Glad to have you back. *(Shifts, looks at Nya with concern)* Afternoon, Nya.

NYA *(Dryly)*: Hey, Dun.

DUN: How you doin' today?

NYA: Survivin'. Like every day.

DUN: Good for you.

NYA: Yep.

(Dun goes to the freezer. Pulls out a frozen meal and sticks it in the microwave.

Nya sits at the table and pulls out a stack of papers. She begins to sort through and check them.)

DUN: Careful in the lot today after work. They been jackin' cars again.

LAURIE: Still haven't deterred those bastards?

DUN: Not yet. Principal Colden says we're working on getting more surveillance.

LAURIE: What the hell's the point of the security cameras they put in if it's not going to scare off these hoodlums?

DUN: I'm gonna be stationed out there from twelve to three P.M. Don't worry. I won't let 'em lay a hand on your Benz, baby.

LAURIE: Fuck you, funny man. My shit Oldsmobile hasn't failed me yet. Like having an ugly faithful husband. Nobody wants him but me and that's good for us.

DUN: Nothin' wrong with your car, baby. Got character. Just like you.

(Laurie stands up and discards her lunch scraps.)

LAURIE: Well that's enough socializing for me. I've got to get my room intact 'fore the next set of hooligans comes in.

DUN: You need me to come up there for any reason, you know how to buzz me. I got you on priority.

LAURIE: Don't worry about me. Take care of these young gals who don't know shit about how to fend for themselves. Me? I'm an old dame. A little reconstructive surgery and I'm back in the game.

DUN: Got it, mama.

(Laurie walks to the door. Takes a strange and revealing inhale.)

LAURIE: This is my den, you know? This is always my den.

(She exits into the hallway.
Dun looks at Nya, who has been buried in her papers.
He eats silently. She ignores him. Then finally:)

DUN: You been all right?

(Nya looks up, faking surprise.)

NYA: You talking to me?

DUN: Nobody else here.

NYA: You don't need to do this.

DUN: What's that?

NYA: Make small talk. Check on me. Pretend to give a damn. Really. I've got lots on my mind and lots to do and I don't need to fill the space. I'm cool with the emptiness.

DUN: Guess you are.

NYA: What?

DUN: Nothin'.

(Pause. Nya tries to go back to her papers. She's too distracted.)

NYA: You got a smoke?

DUN: Can't do that in here.

NYA: I'm going to take it outside.

DUN: Don't wanna have to bust you.

NYA: You being funny?

DUN: Will it make you smile?

NYA: I'm out of smiles for today.

DUN: That's too bad. What's left for your students?

NYA: Gwendolyn Brooks.

DUN: The poet.

NYA: You know her?

DUN: You think I spend all day guarding a school and some of the knowledge don't rub off on me?

NYA: Lots of folk spend all day in a school and don't learn diddly. It's very possible.

DUN: True dat. But I'm not one of 'em.

NYA: Well that's good.

DUN: So you all right?

NYA: Why do you keep asking me that???

DUN: I want to hear an answer that makes me satisfied.

NYA: I'm not here to satisfy you.

DUN: Didn't say you were.

NYA: Then let it go.

DUN: I never hear from you anymore.

NYA: Don't do this here.

DUN: That never happens to me.

NYA: First time for everything.

DUN: I do something you don't like? You can just tell me. Don't gotta do the cold shoulder.

NYA: This isn't a cold shoulder.

DUN: What is it then?

NYA: Sanity. Coming back to senses. Professionalism. Intelligence. Appropriate behavior. That's what this is.

DUN: You gonna play by the books on me?

NYA: I'm not playing anything. Jesus. I can't do this right now.

DUN: All right. Don't do anything.

NYA: Okay.

(Dun eats. Nya heads to the door.)

Got ten minutes before my next class. You sure you don't have a smoke? I really need it. Today. I need it today.

(Dun reaches in his pocket and tosses her a pack. She takes out a cigarette and places the pack on the table.)

Thanks.

DUN: That's something we do well together, ain't it?

NYA: What's that?

DUN: Vices.

NYA: I don't . . . I guess . . . maybe . . .

(Nya takes an inhale that is revealing, and then exits into the hallway.
Dun stays in the room. Eats an apple. And sighs.)

4

*Nya in class. On the board: the Gwendolyn Brooks poem "We Real
Cool."*

*Omari in undefined space—he and Nya are not visible to each
other but are somehow strangely connected. As he embodies the
words of the poem, the words are magically/profoundly written on
Nya's chalkboard.*

NYA: Class, today we're going to look at one of my favorite
   poems by Gwendolyn Brooks. "We Real Cool. The Pool
   Players. Seven at the Golden Shovel."

OMARI:
   We real cool.

NYA: I want you to look at this poem in both versions that I'm
   sharing with you. Notice its layout.

OMARI:

> *We left school.*

NYA: These are from two publishers. One—HarperCollins, a known white American company. The other—Broadside Press, one of the first major publishers of black revolutionary writers.

OMARI:

> *We lurk late.*

NYA: Revolutionary. *(To student)* Come on, Tiffany, you know what that means. Think about it. Yes, change. Thank you for the assist, Tomika.

OMARI:

> *We strike straight.*

NYA: In the HarperCollins version, the layout is pretty common. Large title. Words at the beginning of each stanza are capitalized. There is almost an attempt to erase the idea that the piece is written in "broken English."

OMARI:

> *We sing sin.*

NYA: But in the Broadside Press version, the font looks like graffiti writing, not what we normally see in our textbooks. *(To student)* That's right, DeShawn. Because graffiti writing reps the hood. I would agree that it doesn't get the same respect.

OMARI:

> *We thin gin.*

NYA: So why do you think this independent black press decided to lay out the poem in this broken graffiti style? What do you think they're saying about structure and rules? What do you think they're saying about the education of the young men in this poem?

OMARI:

We jazz June.

NYA: The pool players in this poem are teenagers. And what if I told you it was the middle of the day on a school day? What are they doing in a pool hall on a school day?

OMARI *(As if getting stuck)*:
We di—di—di—

NYA: Ms. Brooks is talking about something here. She is saying they are skipping school. Hanging around bars and thinning gin. Jazzing June. *(To student)* Yes, June is a girl's name, Darnell. So "Jazzing June" means what? *(A response)* Okay, Paul, I think you can find a better phrase, but "laying that pimp game" will do for now.

OMARI:

We real cool.

NYA: Some people might look at the Broadside Press version and think it's invalid because it doesn't follow the rules of English grammatical structure.

OMARI:

We left school.

NYA: It looks like street writing.

OMARI:

We lurk late.

NYA: But sometimes, rules are meant to be broken.

OMARI:

We strike straight.

NYA: Sometimes the street has valuable lessons too.

OMARI:

We sing sin.

NYA: Ms. Brooks has her own rules.

OMARI:

We thin gin.

NYA: She breaks up the "We's" on each line because she wants us to pause.

OMARI:

We . . . . jazz June.

NYA: She wants us to think about that "We" before the next line.

OMARI:

We . . . . di—di—di—

NYA: Each "We" questions their existence and worth.

OMARI:

We . . . . di—di—di—

NYA: Because who are they? At pool halls. Skipping school. Drinking. Having sex. Hanging late. What will they become???

OMARI:
We

NYA: Gwendolyn Brooks gives us the answer in her last line.

OMARI:
We

NYA: A line that haunts us all.

OMARI:
We

NYA: A line that will be their epithet.

OMARI:
We

OMARI AND NYA:
We die soon.

(*Pause.*
Nya hears herself. And possibly Omari. It is disturbing.)

NYA (*To Omari*): What?

OMARI: I said—
We die soon.

(*Uncomfortable moment. Nya looks around herself. A little hot.*)

NYA: I . . . um . . .

(Nya looks at Omari. But also through him. It isn't literal, but his presence has definitely intercepted this lesson.
Nya looks out. At her class.)

I, um . . . I seem to have forgotten . . . can't find my place in my . . .

. . .

. . .

(Nya stops. Looks out into the class again.
A small and audible gasp. A little admission of failure.
Stillness.)

No, I'm fine, Shawna. Thank you, I—I think that's enough of that for the day, so . . .

. . .

. . .

I'm sorry. I've got to step out for a sec but . . . you can work silently, okay? Work on your own response to this poem. I'm going to step out. Please, don't get out of your seats. Darnell. Paul. I'm serious. Thank you.

(Nya immediately walks out of the class.
A light sharply disappears on Omari and the classroom and reveals Nya outside of the door.
She slumps down and begins to weep uncontrollably. Suppressing the sound of her own cry. Clinging to her composure.
A moment.
Dun appears in the hallway. He notices her and rushes over.)

DUN: Yo, hey hey you all right?

(Nya immediately stands erect and straightens her clothes.)

NYA: Shit. Yes. I'm fine.

DUN: You sure?

NYA: No. Yes. I'm perfectly—

DUN: Cuz if one of those little suckas is in there causing problems, you know you just gotta hit me up, right?

NYA: I'm fine. I can handle my son just fine. I don't need your help.

DUN: Your son???

NYA: My what? I said my students. Why are you—

DUN: Cuz you just . . .

NYA: I have work to do.

DUN: You . . . . okay?

NYA: I'm gotdamn amazing.

(Nya disappears into the classroom. An abyss of darkness. Dun stares after her. Questioning . . .)

5

Jasmine at a dorm. She paints her nails. Puts makeup on. Packs a bag of clothes. An earpiece in her ear.

JASMINE: Our school is fuckin' fucked. Bitches can't never mind their own damn business. Gossip whores at every level. It's like—private school for what? For who? Ain't nothin' you do here private! My parents are stupid crazy paying all this money to keep me away from all the kids in my neighborhood cuz they're so damn spooked I'll get pregnant or shot or some shit if I go to public, but I'm like—they must not've ever been in the staircase here at freakin' Fernbrook cuz for reals . . . it's all types of teen fuckery going on and these rich bitches are the nastiest— straight up. It's like they privilege bought them some extra freak or somethin', or maybe they ain't never known what it's like to be desperate so they rather figure that out through sex or whatever. It's tragic. And I cannot keep myself in this wasteland of talent. Stuck-up girls in my dorm acting like I'm gonna steal their fabric softener or grab their granny panties out the laundry cuz I don't have my own or whatever. Like are you serious? Bitch, I may not have your money, but I have BOTH my mother and father at home workin' their asses off at two jobs just to have me study up here with the rest of you cuz they think your privilege will rub off on me by association or some shit. Or maybe they believe in the false god of this freakin' Fernbrook Academy that somehow it produces better people and I keep trying to explain to them that someone like me would actually survive better in an environment in which I am COMFORTABLE instead of being the token poor girl of color that everyone thinks is trying to sleep with their pussy-ass boyfriend or take their gotdamn cocaine or crystal meth or whatever, meanwhile the worst shit my friends from the block are smokin' is weed. If it wasn't for Mr. Peterson's science class and Omari, I would slit my wrists. That's why I'm goin' after O. He's not leaving me here to rot with these bougie brainwashed brats. I'm followin' my man. You gonna read about this in one of them urban romance novels. It's called ghetto love.

(A knock on the door.)

Yo, I got company—lemme call you back. I got more bitchin' to do. That was only half.

*(She hangs up the phone. Goes to the door.
Fuck. It's Nya. She looks distressed.)*

NYA: Jasmine.
JASMINE: Hi . . . .
NYA: Can we talk?
JASMINE: Okay . . . .

(Jasmine steps aside. Nya enters.)

NYA: I came up to get Omari.

JASMINE: I figured that.

NYA: He was supposed to be here. With his things. Meet him downstairs. But he's not here. Not in his room. Nowhere.

JASMINE: Really?

NYA: You know where he might be?

JASMINE: Sorry, Miss Joseph. I don't know.

NYA: Are you sure?

JASMINE: I'm sure.

NYA: Did you see him at all today?

JASMINE: Earlier. I . . . I saw him earlier.

NYA: And did he seem—upset? Was he himself or . . .

JASMINE: I know what happened. I mean, I wasn't there. Didn't see him actually put his hands on . . . . But I was informed. I was in class at the time. He was having a bad day, I think.

NYA: A bad day?

JASMINE: Sometimes somebody mess with you on the wrong day . . . it's like THEY don't know it's your last straw. But they ain't seen how many times you been sucked of everything you got. They go pickin' at you like lint and be lookin' surprised when you knock 'em flat the hell out.

NYA: Jasmine.

JASMINE: Yes.

NYA: He's my only son. You know?

JASMINE: I know.

NYA: I don't . . . I'm not here to hurt him. I'm here because I love him, and I want to help make things all right. You understand that?

JASMINE: 'Course I do.

NYA: So, I need your help.

JASMINE: Miss, I don't know.

NYA: Okay. I hear that. It's just . . . you're the one he talks to the most. Did you know that?

JASMINE: Am I?

NYA: Absolutely. The most. And if anybody . . . if he would tell anyone his plans . . . more than anyone in the world. It'd be . . .

JASMINE: Me?

NYA: Exactly.

JASMINE *(Almost proudly)*: Wow. That's real.

NYA: Jasmine, I don't want to make a big deal of this to the school right now. He was supposed to get his things and be waiting for me downstairs. This is our normal routine. His counselor left him to go and pack his bags. And now, no Omari. If I ask the school, they're going to sound the alarm. Make more of a problem. And then whatever trouble Omari is in, he'll be faced with more. You understand?

JASMINE: God, Ms. Joseph. They are unreasonable.

NYA: Okay. What does that mean?

JASMINE: He's not a criminal.

NYA: I know that, Jasmine. I don't think he's a criminal either. I just want to know where he is.

JASMINE: Sometimes people push you too far. Make you feel like an animal from another jungle. Like you don't belong even when you're here. Cuz they got expectations that you of the wild. So you become the expectation. But it ain't born in you, know what I'm sayin'. It ain't what you want to be. It's what you become. That's the crazy of Fernbrook.

NYA: Jasmine.

JASMINE: He's my heart, Miss J. I love him.

NYA: Then tell me where he went.

JASMINE: I ain't no snitch.

NYA: Snitch?

JASMINE: I still come from what I come from. This place don't change that.

NYA: Jasmine, you know where he went.

JASMINE: Not exactly anyway.

NYA: What . . . what does that even . . . what does that mean?

JASMINE: I got ideas. If I'm in his head right. But I don't know nothin' for sure.

NYA: Give me some ideas.

JASMINE: I can't do that. Don't ask me. Please, Miss. I'm not his betrayer.

NYA: His betrayer?!?

(Nya breathes. Composes herself.)

I'm . . . trying here, Jasmine. To be calm. I'm trying not to unravel. Unleash.

JASMINE: I don't wanna see you unleash.

NYA: I know you think you're being . . . This isn't an act of loyalty. Not for real. In your head, maybe. But not in reality. In reality, you're sentencing him to . . . . I need to find him.

JASMINE: You look real stressed, Miss.

NYA: I'm very stressed. He's my son.

JASMINE: I understand. I know what it feels like to love him hard. Believe me.

NYA: Do you.

JASMINE: I mean his unpredictability is manic. It's excruciating sometimes. Like nails going straight through the heart muscle. But inside, you know he's like an infant needing some kinda nurture. And there's a sweetness to him that make you wanna give it. Make you wanna give up everything to hold him tight.

NYA: Jasmine, this is not helping.

JASMINE: Did you ever like me, Miss?

NYA: What?

JASMINE: When I'd come over. You hardly ever really . . . it's like you was polite but not nice. I know the difference.

NYA: I don't see what this has to do with—

JASMINE: I'm not trying to grill you or nothin'. I was always just curious. Like if I did something wrong I didn't know about. Sat in your favorite chair once or drank the last of some juice I didn't know was near empty. Like if it was some action of mine or just my presence alone. I would understand either way. I just always wondered.

NYA: Jasmine, I don't dislike you.

JASMINE: Yeah, but you don't like me either, right? I mean, "I don't dislike you" . . . that's like passive-aggressive, sorta. It's not committing to loving or hating. It's almost worse. Like indifferent.

NYA: I . . . don't know you well enough to . . . It's hard to like someone you don't know beyond a few hellos.

JASMINE: Someone smart and cute—most days.

NYA: Still someone you don't really know.

JASMINE: Someone with a heart so big the sky couldn't hold it.

NYA: Someone I'm sure is great in her own way.

JASMINE: Someone definitely great in every way.

NYA: Okay, sure.

JASMINE: But someone also dating your son.

NYA: My only son.

JASMINE: Exactly. Like the way you just said that. That was kinda like . . . I mean that was almost a threat.

NYA: A—what do you mean?

JASMINE: Like—and excuse my language please—but it was like: Yeah, bitch, that's my only son and you trying to take him from me or whatever.

NYA:

> . . .
>
> . . .
>
> . . .

40

JASMINE: I said excuse my language please. I hope you heard that part.

NYA: I heard that part.

JASMINE: Okay.

(Pause.)

NYA: Jasmine, do you have any brothers or sisters?

JASMINE: This like a bonding question? Or an interrogation question?

NYA: Whatever kind comes with an answer.

JASMINE: I'm an only child. Like O. We connect that way.

NYA: I see.

JASMINE: But I have one older cousin and one younger. Both boys. They like brothers to me sometimes.

NYA: You ever know what it's like to care for them? As a woman? Worrying about what can happen to them when they leave out into the world every day?

JASMINE: Um . . . they just my cousins, so . . .

NYA: It's a gamble, Jasmine. All the time. You send your young man out into the world every day, or away for a weekend. A semester. A school year. But you don't know . . . you have no idea if they're safe. You have no idea if one day someone will try to expire them because they are too young. Or too black. Or too threatening. Or too loud. Or too uninformed. Or too angry. Or too quiet. Or too everyday. Or too cool. Or too uncomposed. Or too mysterious. Or just too TOO. You don't know, Jasmine. And it's frightening. It leaves a tremble in your heart on a daily. And if someone could ease that tremble by unveiling just a little piece of the puzzle . . . It would mean everything. You know what I'm— You get me?

JASMINE: Men are a puzzle, straight up. I get you.

NYA: I know you want to protect Omari. I know you care about him deeply.

JASMINE: So deep I got indigestion over him.

NYA: But keeping his whereabouts a secret. That is not helping him. You hear me? Not even a little bit.

JASMINE: What you gonna do if you know? Go follow him? Convince him not to do something he set his mind to? You really think that's possible?

NYA: I wouldn't be worth my salt as a mother if I didn't.

JASMINE: Miss Joseph, I know you think maybe I'm not good enough for your son. My parents think nobody's good enough for me. I get it. Nobody's good enough for nobody. But me and Omari, we got something real and even if you think I'm worthless, I'm still gonna love him.

NYA: I don't think you're worth—

JASMINE: Nah, you do. You don't want to, but you do. I can smell when I don't make sense to somebody. I make you afraid. Just like O makes my parents afraid. It's like you send us here to become these different people. You want us to have so much and you want to protect us from ourselves. You love us and we know that. But you hate us too. You hate us having a mind of our own. You hate that we can't be exactly what you imagined in your head. And that scares you. That we don't belong to you. That someone can come along and we might love them more than we love you. You hate us for that. We can feel it inside and it will make us leave and never come back.

(A moment.
  Nya moves closer to Jasmine. Almost threateningly close.)

NYA *(A chilling tone)*: Where. Is. My. Son.

JASMINE:

   . . .

   . . .

   . . .

(Jasmine and Nya have both nearly stopped breathing. They stare into each other.)

JASMINE:

   . . .

   . . .

   . . .

NYA *(Threateningly)*: Jasmine.
JASMINE: Maybe the train station.

   . . .

   . . .

   Or the bus.
NYA: To go where.
JASMINE: Didn't say. But he said it was goodbye.
NYA: Someone come to pick him up?
JASMINE: Caught a ride with Brian. He told the counselor he was coming up to pack his clothes. They let him go and he . . .

   . . .

   . . .

   Snuck out with Brian.

(Nya gasps.
* Another audible failure.)*

I tried to convince him not to go. To stick out his fate like a man. But he . . . didn't want to be a burden no more. To you.

(Nya's breathing accelerates.)

NYA: Why would he—

JASMINE: They videoed him, Miss. It's gonna go viral. Somebody already sent me a text.

NYA: Jesus.

JASMINE: He thought he'd bring so much shame. He thought he'd ruin you.

NYA: And he didn't mention a place? I need to know now. I need to know.

JASMINE: I'm telling you everything I know. Betrayal all day.

NYA: Think for a minute. I need to know before I leave. I need to know if he mentioned any other place.

JASMINE: I told you what I know for sure.

(Nya eyes Jasmine's bags of clothes. Registers them for the first time.)

NYA: You planning to go home early for the weekend?

JASMINE: Hunh? Um . . .

. . .

. . .

NYA: Jasmine. Do not bullshit me. You planning to meet him somewhere?

JASMINE: I was plannin' on . . . searching.

NYA: Searching where?

JASMINE: The train station. The buses. I swear that's it. I don't have nothin' else. He kept sayin' he had to do this on his own. Had money from his father. Child support stash. Said he would be okay.

NYA: Has he called or text you?

JASMINE: No. I wish, but no.

(Nya walks close to Jasmine again.)

NYA: Listen to me. Listen. If he calls, texts, gets online, or does anything to reach you, you call me immediately. You understand me?

JASMINE: He won't, Miss. You're cut out and so am I.

NYA: Just do what I say.

(Nya storms out.)

6

Nya's living room. Darkness except for one lamp.

> *Nya smokes a cigarette. Pours herself a drink. She is sleepless. Donny Hathaway plays. Nya sips and smokes, interchangeably.*

> *The door rattles. She sits up, alert. The door takes a minute to open. Finally it does.*

> *In walks Omari.*

NYA:

> . . .

> . . .

> . . .

OMARI: I'm back, Ma.

NYA: . . .

> . . .

> I see.

OMARI: I um . . .

. . .
. . .

NYA: Where've you been?

OMARI: With some friends.

NYA: Friends.

OMARI: Was tryin' to catch a bus over to Philly.

NYA: Philly? What were you gonna . . . Philly???

OMARI: My boy Rashad. Got a small crib there. From when his
father passed. Said he had a couch . . . .

NYA: So that's the plan, hunh? Run off and not face any of this.
Leave me here to deal with the mess. That's the plan?

OMARI: It was somethin'. Don't know 'bout a plan.

NYA: Well what happened? Plan go awry?

OMARI: Naw I just . . .

. . .
. . .

(Omari fights the urge to cry.)

I don't know, Ma. I just came back.

NYA: I see.

(A moment of silence.)

OMARI: You been smokin'.

NYA: You've been fighting.

OMARI: I—

. . .
. . .

You wanna hear? Or you even care.

NYA: Don't do that, Omari.

OMARI: Do what?

NYA: Ask if I care. Put this on me. Deflect. That is not going
to float right now.

OMARI: I'm not trying to deflect, Ma. I'm askin' if you care to hear or if you prefer not to hear cuz maybe the details won't make it better right now.

NYA: I always care.

OMARI: I'm not saying you don't.

NYA: Then yes. Tell me the gory details. I want to know what devil got into your hands and made you attack your teacher.

OMARI: You don't understand, Ma.

NYA: Make me.

OMARI: I wanna start by sayin' I'm not justifying. There is no way to—I'm not justifying. But everything I say now is just the how. You know? The how and why. But not the excuse. I'm not making none of those no more. I'm done.

NYA: So give me the how.

OMARI: I couldn't see straight. That's what I know for sure. It's like I went blind for a second. No insight and no outer. I was just trying to get through the week.

NYA: What blinded you, Omari?

OMARI: He kept questioning me. In class.

NYA: Questioning you how?

OMARI: Didn't feel like being bothered. I said that to him, Ma. I told him I wasn't in the mood for being questioned.

NYA: Omari, he's your teacher. He has the right—

OMARI: Nah . . . he don't. Not how he was doin' it. Been doin' it a lot and I was sick of it. We get to discussing the reading. *Native Son*—Richard Wright. And he start asking questions. What made Bigger Thomas kill that woman? What were his social limitations? What made the animal in him explode? And who he lookin' at when he askin' all these questions, Ma. Who he lookin' at?

NYA: Omari.

OMARI: Like I'm the spokesperson. Like I'm Bigger Thomas. Like I'm predisposed or some shit to knowing what it's like to be an animal.

NYA: Omari, watch your mouth.

OMARI: You hear me though? You hear what he doin'? He start picking me out. Askin' me to answer. What did I discover when reading the text.

NYA: He's your teacher. He's supposed to ask you about the text, Omari!

OMARI: Nah, he ain't. He ain't just questionin' me about *Native Son*. He ain't just talkin' text. He sayin' somethin' else. Something beneath the question and it's like I'm the only one who can hear it.

NYA: That doesn't give you the right to lose your cool, Omari. That doesn't give you the right to be the animal.

OMARI: But it's all he seein'. Won't leave me alone. I said, Mr. don't pick on me today. I ain't got nothin' to offer. But he won't leave me alone.

NYA: A teacher is supposed to engage you. Even when you don't feel like it. That's the teacher's job. I've told you that repeatedly.

OMARI: We not talking a teacher doin' their job. We talkin' provoking. We talkin' agitating. We talkin' singling me out. You know that, Ma? On a day where . . . Where I don't FEEL like being singled out. We talkin' respecting my space.

NYA: You're in SCHOOL. You're not in your personal space. You're in a collective space. A space to engage and be questioned and be stimulated and be provoked. That is education, Omari.

OMARI: I'm talkin' biased education, Ma. I'm talkin' disrespect. He knows. He knows he wasn't . . . . he was sayin' somethin'. Asking me. In that room. In that way. In front of all those students. On THAT issue. He was sayin' somethin' directly to me. I know he was.

NYA: Even IF he was, even if . . . what are you telling me? You telling me that makes you attack him? You're trying to draw some perpendicular line here? I'm not seeing where these things cross.

OMARI: I told him to back off.

NYA: You said that already.

OMARI: I told him, Ma. And he kept digging.

NYA: And then???

OMARI: And then he says, Mr. Joseph, your perspective is mandatory here. Tell the class your perspective, or take a zero for the day.

NYA: Still not seeing.

OMARI: You threaten my grades. You threaten to punish me in front of the class because I don't want to be your token responder. That's bullshit.

NYA: Did you also cuss like that? Or are you reserving that disrespect for me personally?

OMARI: I'm sorry. I'm just amped. Making a point.

NYA: You haven't made a point yet. You haven't given any indication for how your behavior was warranted. You haven't done anything but speak as if you're above reproach. And you're NOT.

OMARI: Forget it, Ma.

NYA: No, let's not forget it.

OMARI: No, LET'S. I knew you wouldn't . . . . I knew this was futile.

NYA: This is your third strike, Omari. The worst one. You put your hands on your teacher! You attacked your teacher.

OMARI: I pushed him! I didn't attack.

NYA: You think they care about your semantics?!

OMARI: I pushed him and he fell against the board.

NYA: You slammed your teacher against the board.

OMARI: Now THAT'S some semantics.

NYA: And it's been recorded by students. No one is going to see anything different. Do you understand that?

OMARI: I tried to get up and leave. He wouldn't let me leave. That's unreasonable. I told him I wasn't in the mood. I told him!

NYA: They don't care about your mood!

OMARI: Exactly! They don't care, Ma. They don't care what space and place I'm in. I know me. I know how to learn. I know when I'm good and when I'm not. And I said it. I'm not good. I said that.

NYA: Then you ask for permission to be excused. You say you need to speak to your counselor, immediately. You don't just walk out in the middle of a lesson as if you are some sort of king or god that no one can tame.

OMARI: Tame?

NYA: Damnit, Omari.

OMARI: Tame.

NYA: Do not do that. Do not twist and remodel this convo and change the meaning.

OMARI: I'm not changing anything. I'm repeating. Verbatim.

(Pause. Nya takes a breath.)

NYA: So why are you here?

OMARI: Hunh?

NYA: What'd you come back here for? Had nowhere else to go?

OMARI: I just . . .

. . .

. . .

Ain't wanna leave that way.

NYA: So what is this? This is our goodbye? You coming to tell me goodbye?

OMARI: Ma . . .

NYA: You dropping out? Leaving school? A school your father and I vetted for you. A school that was supposed to—

OMARI: Give me all these opportunities. Make me a better man than I'd be if I just went to your school. If I just stayed here. In our neighborhood. *(Pause)* Don't give me his speech, Ma. Those is his words, not yours.

NYA: Your father thought it'd be best—

OMARI: Better than staying with him. "Omari just ain't survivin' in this neighborhood. He's too smart and could be something, Nya. But not in this hood. Let's send him upstate and out of both of our hair." That's what my father thought. That's where his money is going.

NYA: Don't DO that. Don't speak for him or me or us. Don't interpret. You're lost in translation.

OMARI: I'm not lost.

NYA: You are. Shit. You are.

(Beat. Omari walks over to his mother for the first time. He takes the cigarette out of her hands.)

OMARI: Gonna kill yourself with these.

(For a moment, Nya doesn't move. She allows her son to dictate the space. He cleans up her drink. Puts the cap on a half-finished bottle of wine.)

You celebrating my disappearance?

NYA: Omari—

OMARI: Not funny. I know. But it's like . . . like a homegoing or somethin' up in here. I ain't die, Ma.

(A gasp. Nya exhales against her will. Talk of his death can do that to her. He notices.)

Sorry.

(Pause.)

We should, um . . . get food or somethin', right? I'm
starved and . . . .

. . .

. . .

I'll cook us some pasta.

(Nya walks over to Omari. She grabs his face.)

NYA: What did I do? Tell me.

OMARI: Ma, don't do this.

NYA: I need to know. If I hurt you . . . if I misstepped. If I for-
got too much or didn't know enough . . .

OMARI: Ma, this ain't you.

NYA: I have tried . . . like religiously . . . like an ongoing
prayer . . . to protect you. I have tried to buffer you from
it all. Tried to flee you and free you. Follow instructions
from your father. From other mothers. From my own
mother. From whomever. And I still don't . . . .
I don't have the answer.

OMARI *(Shaky)*: What you want me to say?

NYA: They could press charges.

OMARI: What you want me to say?

NYA: They could take you from me and I wouldn't be able to
stop them.

OMARI: I don't know what you want me to say. I just . . . .
I don't know what.

NYA: I want instructions.

OMARI:

. . .

NYA: I will take a bullet for you. I will suffocate the sun for you.
I will steal the sky for you. I will blind Moses for you. I will
strip the wind and the rain and the forests for you. Before

I let you die or rot or lose your freedom, I will surrender my own. You know that? I would die if you could be born again without this oppressive rage. I just . . . I don't know what to do. I need you to tell me. Tell me how to save you. Tell me how to give you another life. Tell me what will take this failure away. Because I have listened to everyone else. I'm ready to listen to you. Guide me. Give me the answer. Just give it to me and I'll do it. I swear.

OMARI (*With heartbreak*): Ma . . .

. . .

. . .

I don't . . .

. . .

(*Omari falls silent.*
Nya stares into his face. Touching him gently. It is too much for him.
He pushes her away.)

I'm hungry. Gonna cook us somethin'. You gonna eat?

(*He walks toward the kitchen.*)

NYA: I'm going to sit here. And wait for instructions.

(*Omari turns away, and goes into the kitchen.*
Nya clings to sanity.)

7

Images of school-day disruption: kids walking through metal detectors; teenagers smoking weed on the steps of school or somewhere nearby; teen couples up against a wall kissing, in a stairwell getting intimate, etc.
Omari's voice as the images run. He is in undefined space.

OMARI:

We real cool. We
Left school. We
Lurk late. We
Strike straight . . .
We . . . We . . . We . . . We . . .

Strike
Strike
Strike
Strike . . .

(Lights cross-fade from Omari to Nya.
    She is in a classroom, checking papers. It is lunch period.
Over the PA system:)

PA: Ms. Joseph, please call the main office. You have a visitor.
    Thank you.

(Nya rises from her desk and goes to a wall phone. She dials and
listens.)

NYA: Hey, Hasselhoff, it's Joseph. Yes. He is? Really? *(Pause)*
    Um, shit. Shoot. Yes, send him up. Thanks.

(Nya takes a breath. She fixes her hair. Puts on some blush. Goes
for a cigarette. Bad idea. Puts pack away and sprays freshener.
    A knock at the classroom door.
    Nya takes another revealing breath.
    Okay. Now. Go.)

Come in!

(Xavier enters. He is handsome and well groomed.)

XAVIER: Hi, Nya.
NYA: Hi, Xavier.
XAVIER: Sorry to stop by during school hours. They said this
    was your free period. I didn't get your message until this
    morning. Lost my phone yesterday. Had a million clients
    to track down. Marketing accounts went crazy—
NYA: It's fine.
XAVIER: I just took a half day. Left the firm and came straight
    down here.
NYA: Okay.
XAVIER: Can we talk about what's going on?

NYA: Yeah. Sure. Okay.

XAVIER: He hit a teacher?

NYA: Pushed him. Into the smartboard.

XAVIER: Jesus. Why?

NYA: I'm not sure. He was upset. Said he was having a bad day.

XAVIER: A bad day?

NYA: Said he felt harassed by the teacher. More than the other students. He felt targeted and wasn't in the mood for any of it.

XAVIER: That's no excuse.

NYA: I told him that.

XAVIER: Where is he now?

NYA: Home. I think—home.

XAVIER: You think?

NYA: I—yes. I left him at home. He's suspended. They're going to deliberate and decide whether to expel him. And also press charges. That's where we are. Letting it cool over the weekend. I'm hoping some of the steam will blow off and they'll be more lenient.

XAVIER: This is his third strike.

NYA: Yes it is.

XAVIER: They're not going to be lenient with a third strike.

NYA: I'm just hoping. He says he didn't slam the teacher. But on the video, I think it looks like—

XAVIER: Video?

NYA: Yes.

XAVIER: There's video?

NYA: The kids. Phones.

XAVIER: How did they . . . . I thought phones weren't even allowed . . .

NYA: They're not.

XAVIER: Then how in the hell . . . . They're gonna use that against him.

NYA: He wanted to run away. He tried to run away.

XAVIER: This all happen yesterday???

NYA: I tried to call.

XAVIER: My phone. Shit.

NYA: Yeah.

XAVIER: I give you Sheila's number?

NYA: I don't recall . . .

XAVIER: I'll give you her number. Next time you can't reach me, call her. She'll reach me.

NYA (*Not a pleasant thought*): Yeah. Okay.

XAVIER: Damn, O. How did it get to this? How did he get this far over the line?

NYA: I don't know.

XAVIER: He say anything to you? Give you any answers?

(*Nya laughs to herself. Incredulous at this line of questioning.*)

Something funny?

NYA: You think he gives me answers?

XAVIER: I'm just asking. He ought to. He's supposed to answer to you. He's your son.

NYA: He's your son too.

XAVIER: I know that, I— (*Taken aback*) What . . . what is that?

NYA: What's what?

XAVIER: That just felt like . . . a little bit of . . . accusation . . .

NYA: I didn't do that.

XAVIER: No???

NYA: No.

XAVIER: Okay.

NYA: Okay.

XAVIER: Because we said we wouldn't do that.

NYA: We're not.

XAVIER: Co-parenting.

NYA: Yes exactly.

XAVIER: Not a blame game.

NYA: No one's blaming.

XAVIER: Okay.

NYA: It just sounded like . . .

XAVIER: Yeah?

NYA: You said, "He's your son."

XAVIER: Yeah but mine wasn't—

NYA: It just sounded like.

XAVIER: I'm talking about him. You're his mother. I'm saying he's the son. He should be giving answers when he's questioned. He's the son.

NYA: Yes. Right okay. But you said he's my son. Not THE son.

XAVIER: I meant THE son.

NYA: Okay.

(Pause.)

XAVIER: I'm thinking . . . . I'm thinking he needs a change. A big one.

NYA: Yes.

XAVIER: Maybe he should come stay with me.

NYA: You and Sheila.

XAVIER: Sheila still has her own place. That's . . . that's not what it'll be like.

NYA: I don't know about that.

XAVIER: It's important. Maybe they won't press charges if we . . . . if we tell them that we are changing his circumstances. I'll pull him out of Fernbrook. He'll get enrolled in the school in my neighborhood.

NYA: Or he can go here.

XAVIER: Here?

NYA: Yes here. Where I teach. And have been doing so for over a decade.

XAVIER: Not here.

NYA: There are some good teachers here.

XAVIER: The school is failing, Nya.

NYA: Was failing. Not anymore. They divided us into four different sections. We've been doing much better. And that's about student accountability and the school board. That's not the staff here. Not all of us. There're some good teachers here. He knows them. He'll be comfortable. He'll be here and under my watch.

XAVIER: You can't watch him all day.

NYA: Neither can you.

XAVIER: But I can give him a better surrounding.

NYA: Better.

XAVIER: Don't do that. I'm not making judgments. Let's not make it about that. Let's keep it about O.

NYA: It is about O.

XAVIER: You do what you can. I know that. I'm not suggesting you've done anything wrong. But you resist . . . you and him . . . the offers I make. I'm not— You can be proud. You can ride or die for this hood all you want. That's good for you. But that's not good for our son.

NYA: And you know? You know what's best? Sending him away to Fernbrook . . . it didn't stop the rage. You can't solve him from the outside in. Don't you see that?

XAVIER: What does that mean? Outside in? I'm working with the parts I get, Nya. That's all I get access to. He doesn't let me in. That doesn't mean I'm not still active. I work from whatever way he dictates. He always dictates. But he's the son.

NYA: Our son.

XAVIER: And he can't always be the dictator. It can't always be a democracy. Sometimes we have to—and I try but you . . . . it's like we're running two different governments.

NYA: I thought it was co-parenting.

XAVIER: Sometimes it's time—and I'm not saying you don't do your part—but I'm the man. Not you. And he needs a firmer hand.

NYA: That isn't / blame?

XAVIER: Maybe not always have a choice in the matter. Maybe he's had too many damn choices and he doesn't know how to follow a leader. He thinks it's him. But where is he going?

NYA: And you don't think a firm hand will make him suffocate? You think I'm too loose so he's slipping down the pipe? Which grip is best? Please show me. Please. Show. Me.

XAVIER: You always have to do this.

NYA: Do what?

XAVIER: Make this personal. Make parenting our son a personal battle between you and I.

NYA *(Correcting him)*: It IS between you and ME. We made him.

XAVIER *(Defying her correction)*: It's not you and I. It's you and him. Me and him. Us and him. That's the deal. You and I without him does not exist.

NYA: Ouch.

XAVIER: No. Not ouch. You don't get to say ouch.

NYA: I don't get to be hurt? I can't feel pain?

XAVIER: No. You don't get to do that.

NYA: Okay. That's fair. It was partly my fault—

XAVIER: I'm not looking backwards.

NYA: I'm not asking you to.

XAVIER: You broke this. Not me. YOU. *(Pause. Catches breath)* I'm moving on and that doesn't make me a bad father.

NYA: I didn't say it did.

XAVIER: You also didn't tell our son who the real villain is. And he thinks it's me.

NYA: I never let him think you're the enemy.

XAVIER: He thinks it anyway. And now he won't hardly listen to me . . . won't respect me anymore.

NYA: That's not on me. I never . . . . I never bad-talk you. If you're upset with me because of . . . . That's fine. That's fair. But you and him and whatever is broken— that is not me.

XAVIER: Then let him come. Let him live with me. Give me that authority.

NYA: I haven't any to give you. You think forcing him is going to save him, then do it. You want to dictate, try it. You'll have a great rebellion on your hands.

XAVIER: I can handle rebellion. It's you. You're the barricade. When you resist, he can sniff it. And then I become the enemy.

(A moment of surrender.)

NYA: I won't resist.

XAVIER: I'll talk to the school. On Monday. First thing. That's what I'll do. Pull him out of school and ask them not to press charges.

NYA: Maybe they'll listen.

XAVIER: And then he comes with me. That's the deal. That's how we fix this. You agree?

(Nya falls silent. Takes a breath. Deep and painful.)

NYA: How did we get here?

XAVIER: Ask yourself.

NYA *(A painful admission)*: I miss you.

(Xavier feels her words, but he is effective in his masking.)

XAVIER: I can't—

NYA: I know.

(Pause.)

XAVIER: Do we have a deal?

NYA: He will hate us both.

XAVIER: Or maybe just you this time.

NYA: If it saves his life, I'll be the Devil.

XAVIER: Okay.

NYA: But we wait. Until Monday. Until I can tell him myself. Until I can effectively release him.

XAVIER: You call me before you do. I want to be on my way. I want him to have nowhere to disappear to. You understand?

NYA: This is a deal.

(She holds out her hands. Xavier looks at them. Hesitates.
He finally takes them. It is not really a handshake. It is the closest thing to holding each other.
An elongated moment. Time disappears.
Then finally . . . a school bell sounds.
Xavier pulls away from Nya.
He walks out of the classroom.
Nya gasps audibly.
The fluorescent lights dance wickedly.
Shift.)

8

Laurie and Dun in the teachers' lounge.

LAURIE: Don't tell me that shit. That's bullshit.

DUN: You think it's my fault?

LAURIE: Don't tell me you came as fast as you could.

DUN: Laurie, that wasn't me. Okay? I did what I could.

LAURIE: I CALLED. I fucking called and you didn't answer. What do you want me to wait forever? Let them bust their heads wide open? On my watch? I'm supposed to stand back and watch?

DUN: You didn't call right away.

LAURIE: Fuck you.

DUN: You didn't. That's what the kids are saying.

LAURIE: Fuck what the kids are saying!

(Nya enters the teachers' lounge.)

Ask any teacher over here. Ask Nya. She'll tell you. It's
bullshit.

NYA: You two all right?

LAURIE: Do I look all right?

DUN: Laurie's fifth period. DeShawn and Hakeem got in a fight.

NYA: No, again?

LAURIE: You hear that?

DUN: What do you want me to do about that?

LAURIE: She said "again." That means these two have an ongoing beef. It's like the fucking Crips and the Bloods in my
classroom. These kids are at war. You want me to watch
them drop grenades and pretend that shit isn't lethal???

DUN: I didn't make up the policy.

LAURIE: Not protect the civilians???

NYA: Did Colden give you shit about it?

LAURIE: Did Colden give me shit about it? Understatement of
the year.

NYA: I can speak to him. Those two have been at it in my room
too.

DUN: That's not going to help.

NYA: Why's it not going to help?

LAURIE: Because they're throwing me to the fucking wolves /
that's why.

DUN: Because you broke protocol.

LAURIE: There is no protocol in war. There is: Stop Two People From Killing Each Other. That is all.

DUN: The broom?

LAURIE: What is it I should've chosen instead? Please tell me
how an over-the-hill chick is supposed to stop two tall
teenage boys with weightlifting muscles and zero body
fat from pounding each other into oblivion without some
type of force? Please tell me!

NYA: What happened with the broom?

LAURIE: I hit DeShawn!

DUN: She hit DeShawn with a broom.

LAURIE: To save his fucking life. I mean—is that even a factor? Does that even matter?

DUN: I'm not saying it do or it don't. I'm just telling her what went down.

NYA: Shit Laurie.

LAURIE: Shit Laurie?

NYA: Colden knows?

DUN: DeShawn ran out of the room and straight to the office.

NYA: Gotdamn.

DUN: It's gonna be a tough one. That broom—

LAURIE: Was all I had.

NYA: What happened to security?

DUN: We came—

LAURIE: —Late

DUN: —As fast as we could.

LAURIE: He had him on the floor. Banging his head into the floor. Desks were scattering all over the place. Kids were screaming. I called security and the damn line was busy.

DUN: We were on the phone with Bekim. He was complaining about a kid who was high in his room.

LAURIE: And so what the hell is the protocol for busy signal? What am I supposed to do?

DUN: Stand aside till we get there.

NYA: That doesn't always work.

LAURIE: Of course it doesn't work. It's stupid. I've got a room full of kids to protect. And myself. I mean what kind of adult just stands there and watches her students fight? What am I supposed to—he was pounding his head into the floor like this. *(She demonstrates)* Like he would've killed him. Hakeem's head was seconds away from splitting open. And DeShawn was seeing red. I screamed for him to stop but you think he could hear me? He couldn't hear the voice of God in that moment!

DUN: I'm just saying what the protocol is. I'm not saying you were wrong.

LAURIE: Fuck right and fuck wrong. There is only necessary.

NYA: What'd Colden say?

LAURIE: He's talking to the parents. The superintendent. Now all of a sudden everybody who doesn't know shit about what it's like to teach in a classroom is going to be my judge and jury.

NYA: Is there something I can do to help? You need me to talk to DeShawn's mother?

LAURIE: She's the least of my problems. Fucking kids and their camera phones. Is everything a gotdamn YouTube sensation with them?!

NYA: They didn't.

LAURIE: How the hell do they get past security with those phones? Tell me that.

DUN: It's back to me again?

LAURIE: It's a simple fucking question.

DUN: Some stuff gets past. It ain't the airport.

LAURIE: Could've fooled me. What's a metal detector for if it doesn't catch all the metal?

DUN: Cell phones ain't the metal we're most interested in. What can I say.

LAURIE: Don't say shit. To me. Ever again.

NYA: Laurie.

DUN: You keep thinking this is me? You act like I did something wrong. What did I do wrong? Was I not able to answer your call fast enough? When it's only eight of us working four different schools in one building, did I not reach you fast enough? Did I not run from one hallway to another at a speed that makes you satisfied? I'm so sorry. I'm so sorry that while I'm sitting up here, barely breaking minimum wage and dealing with the attitudes of a hundred teens and teachers per minute, that I'm not a suitable servant to your beck and call. I do what I fucking can. I'm not Cox—sitting up here stealing computers from the school lab or Bender—flirting with teenage girls. I'm Dun. I'm the last of the good guys wearing a uniform and greeting kids with a smile when they enter the building. I try to make a sunny day out of shit. And I answer every call I get at the security desk. I do my job, damnit. And this time, Laurie, maybe the job got the better of you. That shit happens. But don't go taking me down with you. You get in trouble, you get early retirement. You wanna know what I'd get????— I do my damn job.

LAURIE: Fuck this job! I gave my life to this place. My entire fucking life!

(Laurie falls into a chair from exhaustion and defeat. A beat.)

DUN: Look, I'm sorry—

NYA: It's not just Laurie. Those boys fight. All the time. I've tried everything. Talking to their parents. Splitting them up on opposite sides of the room. I've tried to stop it, myself. We've all tried.

DUN: You can't stop it.

NYA: Don't tell me that.

DUN: How you gonna stop it if you don't know the source?

NYA: I'm supposed to know a million and one sources?

DUN: Gotta know what they carry in them. The resentment and the rage . . . there's a legacy in that. Source of those fights is older than the bricks of this building but nobody's doing they research. You got a bunch of parents. Teachers. Politicians. Whoever. Trying to understand these kids. But how you gonna understand a book you only skimming?

NYA: I've got to understand! My son's life depends on it. I've fucking tried everything!

LAURIE: Nya, you're doing what you can. You put him in a good school.

NYA: It doesn't matter where I send him to school, nothing's working! He's being sucked into this void and I keep trying to hold onto him, but the force is so strong . . . so magnificent . . . that I have . . . to . . .

(Lights up on Omari in undefined space.)

OMARI:
Strike strike strike

NYA: Hold on firm or I'll lose my grip

OMARI:
Sing sin sin sin

NYA: Hang on tight or he'll start to slip

OMARI:
Thin gin gin gin

NYA: Sacrifice something mightier than my soul

OMARI:
Jazz Juuuuuuuuuune . . .

NYA: Sacrifice something mighty

OMARI:
Weeeee . . .

NYA: Sacrifice

OMARI:
We . . . .

NYA: Sacri—

OMARI:
> *We . . .*

NYA: Sac—

(A moment.)

DUN: Nya?

OMARI:
> *Weeee . . .*

LAURIE: Nya, you okay?

(Nya's breathing becomes rapid and short. She is the only one who sees Omari.)

NYA: I . . .

OMARI:
> *Di—di—di—*

NYA: No.

OMARI:
> *Di—di—di—*

NYA: Don't.
LAURIE: You okay?
NYA: I . . . *(She gasps audibly)* I . . .
DUN: Nya???
LAURIE: She's not breathing.

DUN: Nya???

NYA: I can't—breathe—

OMARI:
>   *We die soon.*

>   *(GASP. Nya looks at Omari in terror. She is the only one who can see him. Clutches her heart.)*

LAURIE: Get the nurse. Now.

>   *(Dun rushes out of the lounge.*
>   *Nya collapses.)*

9

A hospital. Omari and Dun sit.
  The PA system in this space sounds strangely like the school PA.

PA: Paging Dr. Roberts at extension 278. Paging Dr. Roberts at extension 278. Thank you.

(Dun looks at Omari, who taps his foot nervously.)

DUN: You want something?
OMARI: I'm good.
DUN: Sorry about . . . this.
OMARI: Yeah.
DUN: She'll be okay though. They said.
OMARI: Yeah.
DUN: She's tough. That's what I always dig about her.
OMARI: Yeah.

(Pause.

Xavier enters. He stops when he sees Omari and Dun. Omari looks at him, suddenly tense.)

(Under his breath) Pssssh. This nigga.

(Xavier approaches Omari cautiously.)

XAVIER: Hey. How's she holding up? Any word?
OMARI *(Defiant)*: Pssssssh.
DUN: Just holding her for observation.

(Xavier looks at Dun with surprise. Who is this guy?)

XAVIER: I'm sorry?
DUN: Overnight. They thought it was a heart attack but now they say it looks like a panic disorder. Just gonna monitor her overnight.
XAVIER: I'm sorry. I didn't realize you were . . . . have we met?
DUN: I'm Dun. Work with her over at the school. Security.

(Xavier looks at Dun. A flash of dawning comprehension. Recognition. This is him.)

XAVIER: Ah. I see.
DUN: You with the family?
XAVIER: Omari's my son, yes. I'm . . . family.
DUN: Oh okay.
XAVIER: I'm Nya's husband. Ex.

(Dun's dawning comprehension. Tension.)

DUN: Ohhhh.

. . .

. . .

Okay.

XAVIER: Okay.

DUN:

. . .

. . .

. . .

XAVIER:

. . .

. . .

. . .

DUN: I should let y'all . . .

. . .

I'll go down to the cafeteria. You want anything, O?

OMARI: I'm / good.

XAVIER: I got him.

DUN: . . .

. . .

Okay. Cool.

(The tension remains as Dun exits.
Omari and Xavier. Defiance and silence.)

XAVIER: You all right?

OMARI: I'm not the one in the hospital.

XAVIER: I know that. I just meant . . . with all this.

OMARI: Stupid question.

XAVIER: All right. *(Pause)* A panic disorder.

OMARI: That's the hypothesis. Runnin' tests now and shit. Make
sure it ain't deeper.

XAVIER: Thank God she's okay.

OMARI: Thank God.

XAVIER: Might be a long wait. The tests.

OMARI: I'll wait. You don't have to.

XAVIER: That's not what I meant. I just wanted to prepare you for . . . . these tests take time and . . .

OMARI: She'll be straight. I got her.

XAVIER: I know you do.

(Pause.)

She and I wanted to talk with you.

OMARI: Words ain't the medicine right now.

XAVIER: Still. I wanted to talk with you. Find out about this acting-out at school.

OMARI: I already pled my case. Gave her the whole one-two. I'm sure she told you.

XAVIER: I want to hear it from you.

OMARI: For what?

XAVIER: Because I deserve to know.

OMARI: Deserve? Why's that? Cuz you pay for the education? Am I wasting your money? You want me to pay you back?

XAVIER: Yeah maybe. Smart-ass. Maybe.

OMARI: I'll write you a check. You can cash it when hell freezes over.

(Xavier grabs Omari by the collar.)

XAVIER: Don't talk to me like that! I'm your father, / asshole.

OMARI: Fuck off me!

(Omari flinches and jerks out of Xavier's grasp.
A moment. They look around the hallway. People are every-where.
Xavier is a little ashamed. How does it get this far so fast?
Omari fumes. Hurt and angry. They sit in silence.)

XAVIER: Shit.

(Pause.)

We gotta work this out.

OMARI: I'm working my stuff out.

XAVIER: Nah. With me. We gotta work this out together.

OMARI: You quit together a long time ago.

XAVIER: I never quit you.

OMARI: You quit her. You quit me.

XAVIER: I didn't . . . . You don't know what you're talking about. There's adult business you aren't privy to. You need to keep the issues separate. You're my son. I never quit you.

OMARI: She was creepin'. That's the adult business. That's the grown-up stuff I can't handle?

XAVIER: Never mind. Let this go.

OMARI: And you were mean. Cold. Making her feel like shit every day. You was never happy living over here and that wasn't her fault. Mine neither.

XAVIER: I took good care of you. Never missed a payment. Never missed a birthday or first day of school. You never went hungry. Always had a shirt on your back. Money in your pocket. Didn't I do that? Is that my sin?

OMARI: You know most of these dudes want their ol' man in their life so bad. They think it's the missing link to the equation. The last ingredient to understanding their manhood. But what's having you in flesh? Flesh ain't shit. It ain't no different than sperm. It's clinical. It does the biology. It don't do the soul.

XAVIER: The hell you want me to do? You want me to cry and hold you in my arms and rock you to sleep? That's not my gig. I'm still your father. I'm still here.

OMARI: Titles is overrated.

XAVIER: You know what? I don't give a shit if you like me or want to go to the gotdamn basketball court with me or pin a fuckin' tail on my ass—I'm here. I'm the father and you're the kid and that's the law of the land. Like it or hate it. Screw it. I'm here.

OMARI: You ain't here. You there. I'm here. We miles apart.

XAVIER: You're gonna respect me. Don't have to like me. Don't have to enjoy my company. But the respect is non-negotiable.

OMARI: Or what?

XAVIER: You really wanna ask me that?

OMARI: I want to know what if I say no.

(Xavier looks at Omari like the Devil. He moves in close to him. Threateningly.)

XAVIER: Sometimes I want to grab you by the throat and choke the shit out of you.

(Omari stares at his father. Somewhat afraid. Somewhat heartbroken. Tears threaten his eyes.)

OMARI: What's stopping you?

XAVIER: Witnesses.

(Pause. The men are still. Again, people are everywhere.)

OMARI: I was sittin' in class, listenin' to the lesson. Was gonna be a silent observer. Was talkin' about *Native Son*. I had woke up that day thinkin' 'bout you. Hadn't seen or talked to you in weeks but the check came on time. I woke up with that check in my hands and I had a feeling about that. Like I didn't know what to say but I wanted to say somethin' to you. I called you but you didn't answer. So I went to class. Sittin' there listening to the class talk about *Native Son*. About the character Bigger Thomas and who he was and what led him to his act of rage. Teacher kept saying he was "unleashed." I kept thinking—animal. And we discussin' this Bigger Thomas. Discussin' his circumstances and what he comes from and this and that. Single mother. That got brought up. One of the students said he only had his mother. And I'm sittin' there listening to this. On a day where I woke up with you on my mind and tried to call you. Tell you I had this feelin' about getting these checks. Tell you I hadn't seen you in a minute. Wonder where you been. But you didn't answer your phone. So I sat there. Listenin' to single mother poor angry animal Bigger Thomas. And when the teacher come askin' me what I thought . . . I felt like he was sayin' somethin' to me. Like he knew I was sitting there, thinkin' about you, feelin' single mother poor angry animal Bigger Thomas-like. And he start sayin', Mr. Joseph—what made Bigger Thomas do that to that girl? What were his social limitations? What made the animal in him explode? And he lookin' at me. But also through me. And I say, I don't want to talk about it. Cuz all I'm thinking about is you. And how I haven't talked to you in weeks but I get this check on time. Like it's automated. Like the bank sends it to me. And I wanted to know if you even mail it. Like is it even personal. Or is it just robotic routine responsibility. And I'm thinking—who does that??? What kinda nigga just sends checks and calls that fatherhood? And we talkin' Bigger Thomas this and single mother that and limitations and animals exploding and I say DO NOT FUCKING CALL ON ME I DO NOT HAVE THE ANSWER. And he keep pushing me and pushing me. And I stand up to walk out cuz I feel the room gettin' smaller and I'm becoming Bigger Thomas even when I hate this part of the story. And teacher get in my way. Tells me to sit down. Grabs me. Like you grab my arm when you try to play Daddy all of a sudden. When it's convenient for you. And I pushed that bitch. Threw his ass offa me and into the fuckin' smartboard. Threw him like he was the monkey hanging on my back. Like he was YOU. And I'm wishing it was you. I'm wishing I could throw him again. Pound his fuckin' face into the ground. Rip that check up and say VOID. But it wasn't you. It wasn't you I pushed. It was my teacher. But I wished it was you. I wished it was you so bad I had to pee. Almost fuckin' peed on myself right there in front of the class. And I don't know if that is hate or love or somethin' else I was feelin'. But I know why Bigger Thomas did what he did and I hate that I know. But you I hate more. You I hate most of all.

(Xavier is silent as Omari glares at him. Tries to breathe. Can't. He tries to speak.)

XAVIER: You know son, I . . .

(But the words fail him. He tries to breathe again. Like some-one is stepping on his chest.
Mountains and walls and miles between them.
Xavier is defeated.)

When the doctor comes out . . .
   . . .
   . . .
Text me.
   . . .
   . . .
I'm stepping out. Need air.
   . . .
   . . .
And off.

I'm going to step off. Need air from all of this. You don't want me in your life. And I don't . . .

. . .

. . .

I don't know what to do about that. I wish I . . .

. . .

But I don't even know what else to do.

(Xavier walks away. Dumbfounded.
Omari sits in the hospital chair. And waits.)

10

Jasmine in undefined space. Maybe her dorm.

JASMINE: I was gonna leave you this long-ass message, but I'm
not sure you'll even get it. And if you do, I'm not sure
you'll even respond back. I think we're over and it kills
me in a thousand ways. Not because I'll never find love
again. I know we're young. I know I'm cute and I'll find
somebody else. It's a lot of fish in the swimming pool or
whatever. But I'm just sad that this is the end of an era and
it's over before it really began. I don't think I got enough
chances to fuck up and get mad at you and yell and then
make up. I hate that. Every relationship deserves to go
through all the colors of the rainbow. That's how you
know you had something. Deep. Ugly. Beautiful. Whatever. We didn't get to give all our shit a try. But for the
little parts we did have . . . For the parts that made me
want to cut a chick's face for you turnin' your head in her

direction, I want to thank you. For giving me that space. For making me feel room enough to be jealous and mad and whatever. Because I also got to smack you and get it out and then that made me free enough to tell you that I love you. I just really really love you. And I hate you for leaving me and breaking it off and not knowing yourself. I really hate you for being so beautiful and confused. But I'm really glad you aren't coming back here anymore. Because this place can't hold you. This place can't hold none of us. For reals. *(Beat)* And I guess I kinda did leave you a long-ass message anyway. But fuck. You know?

(Lights cross-fade to images of school fights; kids going through metal detectors; police handcuffing teenage boys, stopping and frisking.)

PA: Today, students, we have a special poem being read by our Oratory Speech Winner—Carolina Valdez. Go ahead, Carolina.

(A voice clears its throat.)

PA *(Student's voice)*: "We Real Cool," by Gwendolyn Brooks.

(Lights up on Nya in undefined space.)

NYA: I almost lost it. I almost broke down and stayed somewhere in the between. Nervous breakdown is what most folks call it. Doctors call it panic disorder. I call it my moment of revelation.

(Omari in undefined space.)

OMARI: I'm sorry, Ma.
NYA: All my son's life, I thought there was space for him. A little opportunity and education and he'd be complete.

But, members of the board, I'm here to tell you that I miscalculated. Omari's actions aren't his bag alone. They're mine. All of ours. We didn't carve out enough space. He doesn't belong anywhere. There is no block. No school. No land he can travel without being under suspicion and doubt. No emotion he can carry without being silenced or disciplined. He needed more space to be.

(Student's voice continues underneath. Slow and not necessarily spoken where marked. Just trailing as background music.)

PA *(Student's voice)*:
> *We real cool. We*

OMARI: I messed up, Ma. I think there's something wrong with me and I ain't sure what it is . . .

PA *(Student's voice)*:
> *We left school. We—*

NYA: I want my son to belong.
OMARI: I want to turn myself in, Ma.

PA *(Student's voice)*:
> *We lurk late. We—*

OMARI: I wanna take responsibility. I wanna make you stop smoking and drinking and crying.
NYA *(To Omari)*: No. That's not your— *(To the board)* I want my son to have another chance. Be born again with a slate clean of the baggage. Our baggage. MY baggage.

PA *(Student's voice)*:
> *We strike straight. We—*

OMARI: I want to be better.

NYA: Sometimes I look into his face and I get stuck staring. As if I can see what he will become and the longer I look, the longer his life will be. I want him to find space for his anger. Where it isn't quelled but put to good use. Where he isn't a product of bias or low expectation. I want him to know love.

OMARI: They see me as a monster.

NYA: To feel love from all places.

OMARI: Online, I'm a monster. The people made comments. Say I should be kicked out. Locked up.

NYA: He is a man. Young. Still growing. Not fully anything.

OMARI: Like I'm an animal.

PA *(Student's voice)*:
    We sing sin. We

NYA: He's not an animal.

OMARI: Like they expect I would be.

NYA: You're not an animal. No more than the rest of us are. And if so, we built the jungle.

OMARI: I disappoint you.

NYA: I disappoint you.

PA *(Student's voice)*:
    We thin gin. We

OMARI: I can do better, Ma.

NYA: So, if you please, let me take him from here. Let me find him a different school. Reset and try again. But please don't . . . . don't press charges. Don't lock away what hopes he can become. This rage is not his sin. It was never his sin.

PA *(Student's voice)*:
    We jazz June. We—

NYA: It is his inheritance.

OMARI: I know I can do better.

NYA: And I am here before you to say that I take the blame. It is me. Send me away. Punish me. But my son??? . . . . Not my son.

PA *(Student's voice)*:
We die soon.

NYA: Not my son.

(Lights isolate Omari and Nya. They are now looking at each other.)

OMARI: I been thinkin', Ma. About instructions. About what you said.

NYA: Yes.

OMARI: I wrote 'em down.

NYA: Instructions.

OMARI: Yeah.

NYA: For me?

OMARI: For everybody.

NYA: Like a list?

OMARI: Like a scripture.

NYA: Oh. Wow. I see.

OMARI: You wanna hear?

NYA: I'm dying to hear.

(As Omari speaks: images of young men in handcuffs, walking to school with book bags; school fights begin to blend into a wash of colors.

Gwendolyn Brooks's poem overrides the images. It is a collage of chaos.

Omari's words override them all.)

OMARI:

> One: Hear me out.
>
> Two: Let me chill sometimes.
>
> Three: Know when to back off.
>
> Four: Know when to keep pushing.
>
> Five: Let me have some space.
>
> Six: Don't assume me for the worst.
>
> Seven: Show up. In person.
>
> Eight: Be fair.
>
> Nine: Forgive that I'm not perfect.
>
> Ten—

NYA: . . .

> What's ten?

OMARI: . . .

> I don't have a ten yet. I'm still working on it.
>
> . . .
>
> . . .
>
> . . .
>
> These good so far?

NYA: . . .

> . . .
>
> . . .
>
> Yeah.
>
> . . .
>
> . . .
>
> . . .
>
> So far . . .

(Nya touches Omari. She grabs his face and looks into it deeply.
Studies him for all the answers.
> *The moment lasts a lifetime.)*

END OF PLAY